Guiding Lights

Edited by
Claire Tupholme
& Lynsey Hawkins

Stars In Their Eyes

Ellen MacArthur

eline Pankhurst

nce Nightingale

Young Writers

Positive Poetry by Brownies & Guides across the UK

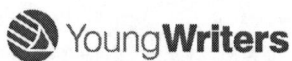

Young Writers

First published in Great Britain in 2006 by:
Young Writers
Remus House
Coltsfoot Drive
Peterborough
PE2 9JX
Telephone: 01733 890066
Website: www.youngwriters.co.uk

SB ISBN 1 84602 462 5

Foreword

Young Writers was established in 1991 to promote the written word amongst school children. Now, in 2006, we are still encouraging children to put themselves forward and to challenge their own talents, especially through specifically tailored themed projects such as our 'Guiding Lights' competition.

This heart-warming poetry collection has been a great opportunity for the young writers involved. Not only has it given them the chance to have their work published, but also enabled them to express who their inspirational figures are through the power of words, creating this thoughtful and heartfelt poetic tribute.

Each piece was chosen on the basis of imagination, perception, technical skill and creativity. The work produced varies from thank yous for help and guidance from close family members or friends, to emotional tributes to people who have suffered but have never given up and have therefore been an inspiration.

We've published the very best of a great selection received, to make this a unique anthology, encapsulating many different images of what an inspirational figure means to young people in today's modern world.

Contents

Chloe Spalding (7)	40
Sophie Lovat (8)	41
Naomi Guzder (9)	42
Hannah Price (7)	43
Rebecca Lidstone (8)	44
Paris Trezise (7)	45
Lauryn Stewart (8)	46
Molly Hurley (8)	47
Ciar Egan-Savage (10)	48
Maisie Prior (12)	49
Megan Sumner (15)	50
Chloe Wheatley (12)	51
Kirsty Ryan (13)	52
Rhiannon Stubbs (14)	53
Pia Davison-Hempsall (12)	54
Katie Ashford (10)	55
Gemma Martin (12)	56
Lauren Chambers (10)	57
Debz Moss & Charlie Hayward (16)	58
Becky Sullivan (13)	59
Clare Hunter (17)	60
Sophie Cooledge (8)	61
Siobhan Keighron (10)	62
Gemma Maxwell (12)	63
Anne-Marie Allen (12)	64
Michelle Allen (11)	65
Ellie McGeary (11)	66
Olivia Voyce (11)	67
Laura Duffy (12)	68
Lizzie Cave (9)	69
Lydia Carpenter (9)	70
Anna Nesporova Newman (8)	71
Kate Dunkley (8)	72
Mollie Burge (9)	73
Paige Lole (8)	74
Molly Symes (9)	75
Daisylea Perry (8)	76
Molly Heath (9)	77
Hannah Hubbuck (8)	78
Molly McCaffrey (9)	79
Loryn Davison (8)	80
Melia Ewart (9)	81

Courtney Benson (8)	82
Laura Bell (8)	83
Lauren Kenny (9)	84
Emily Wilkinson (7)	85
Rebecca Marrs	86
Shannon McCormick (9)	87
Emily Smith (11)	88
Jessica Annett (11)	89
Claire Arch (13)	90
Laura Jones (11)	91
Steph Gostling (13)	92
Molly Pritchard (9)	93
Victoria Hare (10)	94
Stephanie Camy (9)	95
Hannah Maloney (7)	96
Georgina Pritchard (7)	97
Rebekah Corner (10)	98
Kirsty Huggins (11)	99
Kate Rowbotham (12)	100
Lucie Baillie (10)	101
Charlotte Balls (8)	102
Laura Gibson (9)	103
Elise Reid (9)	104
Bethany Lark (9)	105
Imogen James (11)	106
Coral Herbert (11)	107
Jessica Stuart-Smith (13)	108
Ciara Mole (9)	109
Alana Sullivan (7)	110
Tilly Doherty (7)	111
Megan Griffiths (11)	112
Jenine Chue (11)	113
Jessica Button (11)	114
Courtney Healy (10)	115
Annabelle Lee (7)	116
Hannah Corless (8)	117
Kirsty Brooks (10)	118
Megan Faragher (12)	119
Heather Booth (12)	120
Hannah Leece (12)	121
Kelly Firth (11)	122
Abigail Swayne (11)	123

Alusia Malinowska (10)	166
Megan Clapperton (8)	167
Emma Fulton (10)	168
Amy-Leigh Quantick (10)	169
Ellie Smith (13)	170
Abbie Neal (7)	171
Anna Creegan (10)	172
Catriona Cormack (9)	173
Clara Hernon (8)	174
Danielle Sams (9)	175
Ekaete Bassey (9)	176
Georgia Paes (9)	177
Jessica Owusu-Bekoe (9)	178
Kathleen Ryan (7)	179
Lizzie Hay (9)	180
Laura Akehurst (9)	181
Madeleine Hay (8)	182
Megan Nassé (8)	183
Nishoba Kugarajah (8)	184
Tara Nassé (9)	185
Sian Gillespie (9)	186
Aislinn Harkin (9)	187
Jessica Goodman (11)	188
Maddie Lammas (11)	189
Rachel Miller (13)	190
Rachel Eberle (13)	191
Jennifer Meads (14)	192
Maisie Marshall (12)	193
Candi Gilroy (13)	194
Hayley Jones (12)	195
Eleanor Ross (8)	196
Abigail Price (9)	197
Charlotte James (9)	198
Emma McQuaide (8)	199
Jodie Baker (9)	200
Victoria Sidaway (9)	201
Grace Jones (8)	202
Elizabeth Bowater (7)	203
Jemima Cooper (9)	204
Leah Pearson (7)	205
Kathryn Wright (8)	206
Charlotte Oliver (9)	207

The Poems

Young At Heart

(About Barbara)

She may be old or going grey,
Getting slower, day by day,
Becoming weak but still staying strong,
Everyone sighs but there's nothing wrong.

Her life hasn't always been okay,
Her husband died, her son's away.
Her nephew's bullied, his mum's gone,
But still she continues to hold on.

When the care home calls, she doesn't mina,
She moves in but explains she's fine.
She has fall after fall but still stands tall,
She knows she's got to hold on just that bit more.

As time goes by we visit more,
Always knocking on her door,
Amazed at what she's living for
A great person and a family core.

Her nature is what inspires me most,
A guiding light for all those lost,
Her heart is pure, her soul is soft,
So we try and forget that growing cough.

Hannah Mead (13)

Congratulations Hannah – your poem is the first prizewinner! You win a £25 voucher for yourself and a fantastic £1,000 cheque for your unit!

My Sister

(For my sister Danielle)

I love my sister with all my heart,
She is the horse to my cart.
She makes me laugh when I want to cry,
When I'm by her side, I can touch the sky.
She cheers me up when I am down
And she never has a frown.
I love my sister with all my heart,
She's the horse to my cart.
Like when we're having fun
We never get things done.
She's the best thing I've ever had
Even though she thinks I'm mad.
I love my sister with all my heart
She is the horse to my cart.

Chloe Bradley (9)

£25
Prize

Well done Chloe. We chose your
poem as one of the two runners-
up from the competition. You win
a £25 voucher for yourself.

My Inspiration

My mom, she inspires me each and every day
She will always guide me on my way
My mom's always been there through thick and thin
She cheers me up when I'm down and always makes me grin
I look up to my mom like a flower to the sun
My mom is like a mate - fab, funky and fun
Tears, happiness, sadness too
My mom has always helped me through
She makes me feel on top of the world
And always makes me smile
Me and my mom have fun practically all the while
We have a special bond and never will it break
My mom is number one, absolutely, no mistake
She is so great, like no other
She's the world's best, most inspirational mother.

Jade Smedley (13)
3rd Willenhall Guides

Jade, your terrific poem was
chosen as the second runner-up
from the competition. You also win
yourself a £25 voucher.

£25
Prize

My Teacher

My teacher, she is kind.
My teacher, she has a very imaginative mind.
My teacher, she knows lots of stuff.
My teacher, she sometimes huffs and puffs.
My teacher, she gives us lots of work,
And gives us stars as a perk.
My teacher, she is the best,
So at school, I am never a pest!

Annabel Buxton (8)
2nd Oxted Brownies, Oxted

Roald Dahl

He was smart, he was kind,
Every book came to his mind.
'Matilda', 'The BFG', 'The Witches'
'Charlie And The Chocolate Factory'.
And there are no ditches.
In his knowledge on how to write books,
All it needs is imagination, not looks.
I was inspired to write by him,
Inspiration covered me, limb to limb.

He was a book genius,
He liked writing plus.
He wrote poems as well,
So that you could tell
How mean a bad guy was.
Like Aunt Spiker and Aunt Sponge because,
They sound the way they look
And you want a bad crook.

Jessica Lyn Bonsall (9)
6th Portsmouth Brownies, Portsmouth

Who I Admire

Funny and kind, soft and cuddly
Happy, kind and very bubbly.

Plays the piano very well
Good at joking, very swell.

The person that I admire is my dad,
I think that we had a lot of good times together
That's my dad.

Gemma Pay (12)
1st Northfleet Guides, Northfleet

My Role Model Is Sophie Whittaker

Sophie is my role model because
She is so funny and stupid too.
She is always hyper?

She is so caring
She understands your problems.
Every day she is the same
The same brilliant person.

Sophie is the best helper
If you get stuck with work,
She helps and understands you
In every single way.
I could never last without her.
Through my days that I live,
She is the best friend in the entire world,
That's why Sophie W is my role model.

Byrony McFarlane (11)
2nd Brayton Guides, Selby

Sandie The Hamster

Sandie the hamster
and I was his master
Eating and sleeping
and also that squeaking.

Then unfortunately he died,
it was a depressing surprise.
No more hiding under the chairs
or climbing up the stairs.

I remember his paws
but never liked his claws.
He had lots of hair
which, was very fair.

So that's Sandie the hamster
and I was his master.

Nicola Fairbairn (10)
1st Alloway Guides, Ayr

My Mum

My mum is the best
She understands and cares
About me and my family.
She is the best in the world.

She helps me through the good and bad times,
Nurses me back to health,
Helps me with my school work.
She is the best in the world.

She gives me pocket money,
Styles my hair.
She is very protective over me,
She is the best in the world.

Melissa Ring (12)
1st Gillingham Guides, Brompton

My Mate - Jemma

My mate Jemma loves to sing,
So do I but I just swing -
Back and forth, back and forth.
Jemma goes in singing at competitions
And never comes fourth.

Jemma has a dog called Benji,
We call him Benji Wenji.
I have a rabbit called Carlie
He likes to crunch on his barley.

We share the same interests,
We both are pests.
Our parents are not pleased,
Especially when we sneezed.

We both go to Brownies,
Even though we're not 'townies'.
We wind-up our leaders,
Who are common readers.

Philippa Sawkins (10)
5th Radcliffe Brownies, Manchester

Hayley Westenra

H er voice has got to be the best,
A lovely voice she has
Y ou might have seen me in the press
L ooking at her on the stage
E very day I listen to her
Y ou might have heard her songs yourself!

Melissa Roberts (8)
1st Meole Brace Brownies, Shrewsbury

Annie

Annie is a ballet dancer
she teaches me to dance.
She has blonde hair
and walks like a swan.
She is quiet and kind
and moves very gracefully.
She is beautiful
I would like to be Annie
and dance like her in Swan Lake.

Annie wears pink
and has special shoes,
that you can stand on your tiptoes.
Her legs are tall and slim,
we put magic glue on our legs
to stick them together.

Annie is beautiful,
I think she must be a swan.

Maisie Rutter (7)
1st Meole Brace Brownies, Shrewsbury

My Dance Teacher

My dance teacher Lyndsey teaches us to dance,
We jump around and prance.
She's very clever and flexible,
When we go to dance we learn lots
Of new things and routines.
It is really fun.
Lyndsey is fit and kind
And if you don't understand a step
She will help you and go over it again.

Molly Rutter (8)
1st Meole Brace Brownies, Shrewsbury

My Mum

My mum's cuddly
My mum's nice
She'll look after me
for the rest of my life.

When I'm sad
or feel bad
She'll be there
ready to care.

She'll help me out.
No doubt!

Abigail Morris (10)
1st Meole Brace Brownies, Shrewsbury

Who I Admire

Lindsay Lohan is an actress, I want to be like her,
She was in The Parent Trap and played twin sisters.
One of them was Hallie,
The other one was Annie,
She had to learn both of their lines and I admire her.

She has long red hair and freckles on her face,
In Herbie Fully Loaded, Lindsay has a race.
Her car was number 53,
If you watch Herbie, you will see.

I want to be like her because I would like to act,
I think I am good at it, that's a fact.
I would be on TV
On a show, maybe starring me!

Elsa Maughan (9)
1st Dodleston Brownies, Chester

My Friend . . .

My friend is a special friend,
She's always there for me, when I'm feeling low.
She's a friend, I'll always know!
She's bright and she's funny,
She's crazy and she's kind.
She's a friend I'll never forget,
She's always on my mind.
She knows who she is!

Beth Jenkins (9)
1st Dodleston Brownies, Chester

My Mum Is The Best!

My mum is the best in the world because;
She's kind, she's helpful and guesses the weather,
But I don't want to *brag!*
She's funny, she's clever and very good at cooking,
But I don't want to *brag!*
She's good, she's pretty and good at caring for people
But I don't want to *brag!*
You see this is why my mum is the best in the world to me
But I don't want to *brag!*

Lizzie Hough (10)
1st Dodleston Brownies, Chester

Heather

Heather is my riding instructor and she inspires me,
She is the greatest rider and far beyond me.
She is the teacher I have every week
And helps me on my way to being as good as she is and
Hopefully I will reach that, one day.

During my riding lesson, Heather never gives up on me,
We canter and we jump and she's there all the time
To guide me all the way and encourage me to be
As good a rider as she.
So three cheers for Heather,
She is the best, and whether children are big or small
She's heaps above the rest.

Eleanor Hassall (8)
1st Dodleston Brownies, Chester

My Sister

Dawn likes her horse
And so do I of course.
She's a lot older than me
And a horsewoman I would like to be.
She has been in lots of races
I would like to be one of those winning faces.
As she mucks out day and night,
Those are the things that give me a fright.
I know I will need to do my best
And there will be no time to rest.
With hard work and exercise
I will need to build up my thighs.

Charlotte Handley (8)
1st Dodleston Brownies, Chester

Kelly Holmes

Kelly Holmes is my hero
She's certainly no zero.

Across the ground she seems to flow
No one could ever call her slow.

One gold medal would do most,
But twice she passed the winner's post.

No need for Kelly to jump-the-gun
She'll try and try and run and run.

She's the greatest, the best, it's no mystery
In Athens, she ran and made history.

Eleanor Simpson (11)
2nd Hale Methodist Guides, Altrincham

My Granny

She's a bouncy sofa,
She's a cuddly bear.
She's a bright red door, always open,
She's a chirpy robin.
The smell of sweet roses,
A green fingered granny.
A funny clown, always happy,
A colourful sunset,
A musical piano.
A cup of frothy hot chocolate,
A brave warrior,
She's always there for me!

Penny Silverwood (11)
2nd Hale Methodist Guides, Altrincham

Untitled

My dad is a kind, gentle and playful dad,
I love to play with my dad.
My dad has a big heart full of love,
I fit right inside with my mum and brother.
I love the way my dad helps me
And gives up his time for me.
My dad goes to work every day
To make money for our family.
My dad loves to play football,
He also plays football.
I love my dad.

Alice Gill (10)
2nd Hale Methodist Guides, Altrincham

Untitled

I really enjoy
playing with my sister Kaylee.
I love her very much
I like it when she reads to me
And I like her being nice.

Kirstin Flett (5)
1st Dounby Rainbow Guides, Orkney

Laura

M y first swimming lesson was very scary,
Y et Laura would not let me out.

S inging favourite songs to make us happy
W heels on the bus, spinning round and round.
 I learned my breaststroke, arms and legs
M y rubber ring deflated, now froggy float fun,
M y confidence rising, Laura praised me on.
 I can do it! My first 5m swim!
N ow I love the water, many badges in my room.
G et ready to dive! Laura calls.

T here's still so much to learn
E very stroke; butterfly, breaststroke and crawl.
A t times impatient, frustrated but never cross.
C hoosing different ways to make it fun.
H er smiles and giggles always encourage.
E very lesson she makes exciting.
R eally Laura's my number one.

Rebecca Luke (8)
1st Windlesham Brownies, Windlesham

My Auntie Mandy

My aunty Mandy
She's as sweet as can be
And she gives me sweets
And takes me swimming.
She reads me some stories
When I stay over there,
And she takes me out
When I have nothing to do.

Sophie Crow (7)
2nd Belvedere Brownies, Belvedere

My Teacher

My teacher is kind
My teacher is nice
She helps me with maths
She helps me with literacy
She helps me when I'm sad
My teacher plays the guitar.

When I grow up
I want to be a teacher
Just like her.

Amy Underwood (7)
2nd Belvedere Brownies, Belvedere

My Teacher

My teacher is called Mr Greenwood
But for this week and next week
Someone called Mr Lee is teaching.
I like Mr Lee, he is kind
We do lots of stuff with him
Like maths, literacy and topic.
In maths, literacy and topic
It is all fun.

Amy Hutchinson (8)
2nd Belvedere Brownies, Belvedere

About Mrs Paul

I really like my teacher
Even though she shouts.
She gives really nice cuddles.

I really like my teacher
Her name is Mrs Paul,
She always makes me smile.

I will never want to leave her,
I like her to bits!

Lily Solomon (7)
2nd Belvedere Brownies, Belvedere

My Mom

My mom is my idol
She's always there
She gives me love and also came
Whenever I needed her.
She's always around
You can feel her warmth
It always surrounds me
She's there through my tears
My pains and my hopes
She can go through anything
She always copes
And that's why my mom's
My idol.

Leah Sprason (13)
2nd Sutton Coldfield Guides, Birmingham

My Family

My family are caring,
Loving and kind,
They may be daring
But I don't mind.

Sophie Hedley (10)
2nd Sutton Coldfield Guides, Birmingham

Animal

A n animal is to comfort you when you're feeling sad,
N ice and warm and furry, it makes me feel glad
I nside and out I love them, they love me.
M e and my animal belong together it's really plain to see
A ll around is our love
L ove that comes from the skies above.

Elizabeth Wright (11)
2nd Sutton Coldfield Guides, Birmingham

My Family

My family are helpful and kind
If I'm ill they never mind
They're rushing here, rushing there
Rushing everywhere
But they still look after me.

Grace Chew (10)
2nd Sutton Coldfield Guides, Birmingham

My Idol

My idol is my friend
She is there for me
And always helps me
She stands up for me
Through my tears and doubts
Through my hope and happiness
She is my sister
She is my friend
She will be the person I care about
Till the end.

Laurie Jordan (13)
2nd Sutton Coldfield Guides, Birmingham

Family

F or always being at my side
A nd taking me out for a ride
M aking me happy when I'm sad
I t's never the same without my mom and dad
L ike to spend money on me
Y es it's great to have a lovely family.

Danielle Edmonds (11)
2nd Sutton Coldfield Guides, Birmingham

Untitled

Have you ever had a time when everything's right
And the family isn't uptight?
Well that happened to me,
Perfect it may be.
The person I am talking about changed all that,
You must think she is a right old bat.
The person I look up to
Will never let me do
Something I will regret or forget.

Steph Clarke (13)
2nd Sutton Coldfield Guides, Birmingham

The Mother

The figure of a mother,
That is my idol.
Caring and a lover,
That is my idol.

She loves me dearly,
That is my idol.
You can see that clearly,
That is my idol.

She goes through pain, sorrow and tears,
That is my idol.
She takes away my frights and fears,
That is my idol.

She has loved me through all the years,
That is my idol.
She'll carry on loving me as the future nears,
That is my idol.

She is my mum, but she may be rough,
That is my idol.
Lisa Miner, she's brilliantly tough,
That is my idol.

Lauren Miner (13)
2nd Sutton Coldfield Guides, Birmingham

Best Friends

B e a true friend!
E verlasting!
S top arguing!
T rue friends, forever!

F orever friends!
R eliable friends!
I ncredible friendship!
E ndless trust!
N ever argue!
D elightful, together, forever!
S pecial friends!

Jessica Notman (9)
1st Kingsbury Brownies, Tamworth

My Dad

This poem's about my dad,
He is a lad.
I am glad
That he is my dad.

My dad plays with me,
He takes me places that I see.
He works at TNT,
I love my dad and my dad loves me.

Abbie Howe (8)
1st Kingsbury Brownies, Tamworth

My Friend Georgie

I look up to my friend like I look up to my mum
When me and Georgie are together it is so much fun.
We make up plans together and we're always bestest friends,
Until the end of eternity our friendship never ends.

We're best friends for life and best friends for real,
When we are together it's only happiness we feel.
We go to each other's houses and have sleepovers,
But the symbol of our friendship is the lucky four leaf clover.

Hollie Eustace (9)
1st Kingsbury Brownies, Tamworth

About Chloe

Chloe is great
An awfully good mate
We have lots of fun
Dancing in the sun!

I go round her house
We're as quiet as a mouse
And sometimes we are bad
Sometimes we are sad
That's the thing about Chloe
She's lovely and showy.

Chloe Spalding (7)
1st Kingsbury Brownies, Tamworth

My Friend

My friend is someone special to me.
I can see,
She's always been kind to me.

Sophie Lovat   (8)
1st Kingsbury Brownies, Tamworth

Best Friends

Beth, Mia, Sally and me,
We're all friends,
You will see.

We never split up,
If you think that then
Shut up!

We always play together
In the playground
And forever.

Beth, Mia, Sally and me,
We're all friends,
You will see!

Naomi Guzder (9)
1st Kingsbury Brownies, Tamworth

People Who Inspire Me

There are lots of people in the world
There are some who are very clever and know lots of maths
There are some who are very brave and take lots of risks
But there is one person who I always look up to
And that is my mum, for all the things she can do
She helps me with my schoolwork when I find it hard
And picks me up when I fall on the yard
And makes me smile when I'm sad.

Hannah Price (7)
2nd West Brownies, Newport

Grandad Jimmy

My grandad Jimmy was the best,
He always loved me, even if I was a pest.
He let me jump from chair to chair,
He let me play just anywhere.
He said I was his favourite girl,
His little precious, special pearl.
My grandad Jimmy wasn't well
And sometimes on the floor he fell.
He had to go to the hospital, his leg was bad,
He needed an operation, this made me very sad.
My grandad Jimmy has gone to Heaven,
Where all the flowers grow.
He's keeping an eye on me,
My mummy tells me so.
Goodbye Grandad Jimmy,
I still miss you lots.

Rebecca Lidstone (8)
2nd West Brownies, Newport

My Mum

My mummy is special.
My mummy is kind.
My mummy is always on my mind.
She helps me out when I am stuck
My mummy brings me good luck
I love her and she loves me
Together we are as happy as can be.

Paris Trezise (7)
2nd West Brownies, Newport

My Dad

My dad is big and strong
He makes me laugh all day long
For his job he is a taxi driver
At the end of the week
He gives me my pocket money, a fiver
As a treat he takes me to the park
We play kickball and laugh
Bedtime comes and he tucks me in tight
And makes sure I am safe and warm
My dad is the best I know
I'm right.

Lauryn Stewart (8)
2nd West Brownies, Newport

The Queen

The Queen is very smart
She is very nice and kind
She wears long red dresses
And they are very nice
She looks after her country very well
She treats people very nice
She shows everyone how they should be.

Molly Hurley (8)
2nd West Brownies, Newport

Clover My Rabbit

C uddly
L oved
O utstanding
V ictorious
E ntertaining
R uthless

She has been through ups and downs
And bumps and bounds
From just sitting in a little hutch
She has been from scared to happy
Happy to sad
And she is just a rabbit.

Ciar Egan-Savage (10)
2nd Cheadle Heath Guides, Stockport

Kate Moss

Spotted at JFK airport only 14 years of age,
In Style, Vogue . . . she's on the front page
Contracts with companies,
Adverts with Rimmel,
Billboards with her face,
Selling Coco Chanel.

What will all the paparazzi say?
When she Gucci 'ponys' down the runway,
The drug incident didn't bring her down,
She's on the latest catwalk,
In a Ben Di Lisi gown.

Dior, McCartney, Chloe, French Connection,
Kate Moss, the model of ultimate perfection!

Maisie Prior (12)
1st Enderby Guides, Narborough

She

She's gone through times
Both good and bad.
She went off track,
She too went mad.

Though times were bad
She sorted through it.
She learned to love,
Loved life, every bit.

She went to college,
Her mind began to grow.
She then got a job,
It started out low.

She worked her way up,
Survived all the tough,
She grew to be who she was,
And gave to us, all of her love.

Megan Sumner (15)
63rd Cardiff Guides, Cardiff

My Marvellous Mum!

My marvellous mum,
Helps me when I get splinters in my thumb,
She works in the hospital of Heath
And is ready to stop any thieves.

And you just remember,
If you're ever under the weather
Just call my marvellous mum
Heather!

Chloe Wheatley (12)
63rd Cardiff Guides, Cardiff

My Grandad

M akes you want to achieve your goals
Y ou can go to him for advice

G iving me help when I'm stuck
R emembering never to give up
A rtist, never failing
N ever giving up
D oesn't rush anything
A lways remembering his good work
D oesn't stop being kind.

My grandad!

Kirsty Ryan (13)
63rd Cardiff Guides, Cardiff

Jim The Astronaut

He's travelled up and out of space,
Months and years it must take.

He's seen the world from afar,
The sun, the planets and the stars.

Working as a team is an important role,
It must have been his greatest goal.

His job must be a fascinating one,
The one that people have wished they'd done.

He thought of the wonders of the worlds beyond,
Thought of his dream and made it come true!

Rhiannon Stubbs (14)
63rd Cardiff Guides, Cardiff

Miss Earnshaw

Can you paint a rainbow
From the colours in your heart?
Can you feel separate
As the colours split apart?

Red is for anger, the place she never goes,
Blue is for sadness, the feeling she does not show.
Gold is for her beaming face,
Silver is for her loving grace.

She teaches me her wisdom of pen and paint alike,
She teaches me to draw from circle, square and kite.
She shows me the colours, the ones that she knows,
You ask her to paint a picture and off she goes.

Can you paint a rainbow
From ceiling to floor?
She paints the best pictures,
My art teacher, Miss Earnshaw.

Pia Davison-Hempsall (12)
15th Lincoln Guides, Lincoln

Margaret

M argaret is our Guide leader
A kind and thoughtful lady
R eady to help and advise
G uides who need a hand
A kind-hearted lady with a good sense of humour but
R eally strict when needed
E veryone likes her very much
T hat's Margaret, the best there is.

That's Margaret the cool one.

Katie Ashford (10)
15th Lincoln Guides, Lincoln

Mum

Mum is great, she always listens,
She helps you when nothing goes right.
Mum is always cooking my dinner,
She is helpful in every way.
She looks after me when I am ill,
Takes us somewhere special to end bad days
And then when the moon comes up I can feel warm
Warm in love that I keep
So then I can drift to sleep.

Gemma Martin (12)
15th Lincoln Guides, Lincoln

My Best Friend

She is kind
And always there
Helps me if I'm down
She's just like a clown
Light skin and half curly hair
A cheeky grin that you can't miss
She is never tired
And is a bundle of energy
Who can it be?
She's a bit like a clock that never stops
My best friend
Is Stephanie Nock.

Lauren Chambers (10)
15th Lincoln Guides, Lincoln

Mum

You picked me up when I was small
Brushed me down and kissed me better

You used to be my superhero
My saviour and my home

You kept my tears and fears at bay
And chased all the monsters away

You loved me when I was lost
Never gave up on me

You picked me up when I was small
And still do now when I need it much more
You used to be my superhero
Now you're my best friend.

Debz Moss & Charlie Hayward (16)
15th Lincoln Guides, Lincoln

My Ty Collection

Ran into Patti one day while walking,
Believe me she wouldn't stop talking!
Listened and listened to her speak,
That would explain her extra large beak!
Floppity hops here to there,
Searching for eggs without a care!
Lavender coat from head to toe,
All dressed up and nowhere to go!
A proud club member named Clubby II,
My colour is special, a purplish hue,

Take me along to your favourite place,
Carry me in my platinum case!
All good things come to an end,
It has been fun for everyone,
Peace and hope are never gone,
Love you all and say, 'So long!'
Beanie Babies can never end,
They'll always be our special friends.
Start the fun because we are here
To bring you love, hope and cheer!
My world is all about Ty,
All my mum says is my oh my.
All I do is buy, buy, buy.
This is because I collect Ty,
My inspiration is Mr Ty,
On the outside he's just a guy,
But in my mind's eye he's more than that,
He's the aid of my imagination
And he's not fat!

Becky Sullivan (13)
15th Lincoln Guides, Lincoln

Grandad

He was our special grandad, so it's hard to say goodbye
But we know he's better off now, with our granny in the sky
We've got our precious memories, stored up inside our head
Remembering the things he's done and all the funny things he said.

Grandad received a heavenly invitation, as God only takes the best
I hope you all agree with us, that Heaven now is blessed
You've had a good life Grandad, you made us feel so proud
Now we think it's safe to say, that you were the best grandad around.

Clare Hunter (17)
Gosport Senior Section, Gosport

My Teachers

Miss Gibbons takes me for science
Miss Severs takes me for gym
Miss Dimon takes me for English
That's how my day will begin

In science we learn about forces
In gym we do exercises
In English we learn about poems
My day is full of surprises

I learn lots of things from my teachers
My day will end at three
I help pack away all the pencils
Then I can go home for my tea!

Sophie Cooledge (8)
2nd Rowner South Brownies, Gosport

Michael Flatley

Oh Michael Flatley, Michael Flatley,
How you dazzle me!
The way you dance all the time,
You always make me see,
That I can dance all the time,
Oh how you dazzle me!

Siobhan Keighron (10)
4th Fallowfield Guides, Manchester

Emmeline Pankhurst

Thank you Emmeline,
You fought for us,
You saved us from all the fuss,
Now us girls and women can vote,
So I have written this little note.
Thank you!

Gemma Maxwell (12)
4th Fallowfield Guides, Manchester

My Poem For Laura

(I look up to you in more ways than one!)

Laura I wanna say that I look up to you
In more ways than one.
I don't know what I would do or say
When you are gone.
You pick me up when I am down.
Even if I give you a bad frown.
You are very kind and take bad stuff off my mind.
So what can I say, I give you love from above.

Anne-Marie Allen (12)
4th Fallowfield Guides, Manchester

Kirsty Howard

At the age of ten
She fights again
She doesn't fight for herself
She fights for others' health
She holds a brave face
Although she trembles in her place
Still showing a smile
She'll be around for a while
With pride
She'll stay alive.

Michelle Allen (11)
4th Fallowfield Guides, Manchester

Sammi The Greatest

I just wanna say thanks
For setting a great example
You are so kind
You share everything with me
You take everything off my mind.

I love our great sleepovers
When we do our makeovers.

We dance, dance, dance
When we've got a chance.

We love R 'n' B
So now, you see . . .
Why you are the best
Even though . . .
We always make a mess!

Ellie McGeary (11)
4th Fallowfield Guides, Manchester

Shaun Wright-Phillips

Shauny Shauny - your skills so fine
Shauny Shauny - your goals are better than mine.

You kick the ball high in the air
You make the fans just watch and stare.

Your headers, kicks and knee-ups are great
Shauny Wright-Phillips I wish you were my mate.

Olivia Voyce (11)
4th Fallowfield Guides, Manchester

My Memories Of You

As I lie in bed at night
Beneath the dreamy sky,
Full of dazzling stars blinding both my eyes.
I think of you, more ways than one,
As I start to drift away,
Of all the happy memories
That could happen in one day.
The special times I spent with you
Will always stay with me,
No matter where, when or how far
You will know when I think and see.

Laura Duffy (12)
4th Fallowfield Guides, Manchester

Aisha

A isha is good at everything
I nterested in books
S hows everyone her work
H er pictures are brilliant
A isha is helpful and caring.
   I look up to her!

Lizzie Cave (9)
Trull 1st Brownies, Taunton

Midwives

Midwives inspire me,
A midwife is what I want to be.

Midwives look after babies,
Midwives are mostly ladies.

Midwives are kind and caring,
In your joy they're sharing.

Midwives are careful,
Midwives are always cheerful.

Midwives inspire me,
A midwife is what I want to be.

Lydia Carpenter (9)
Trull 1st Brownies, Taunton

My Riding Teacher

H er name is Helen my riding teacher
E ven though she is my riding teacher I would
L ike to be like her because I love horses and
E very pony - they are lovely
N obody can ride like her in the stables.

Anna Nesporova Newman (8)
Trull 1st Brownies, Taunton

Rosie, My Sister

S isters like Rosie are annoying.
I am inspired by her, anyway
S he is my sister and I want her
T eaching me things I want to know,
E xcellent Rosie is.
R osie is my sister and she is great.

Kate Dunkley (8)
Trull 1st Brownies, Taunton

Jacqueline Wilson

Excellent books, such fun to read,
and interesting.
'Bad Girls', 'Midnight', 'Secrets',
all amazing books.
I could read them over and over.
She's so brilliant at writing.
It's almost magical.

Mollie Burge (9)
Trull 1st Brownies, Taunton

Jacqueline Wilson

She writes excellent books,
such fun and so good.
Reading books of an excellent
author is just so cool.
People like her - she is
who I want to be.
An author just for me.
So funny and friendly,
Jacqueline Wilson inspires me.

Paige Lole (8)
Trull 1st Brownies, Taunton

Sue Frankome

I admire Sue Frankome
because she is most amazing
on the flute, saxophone and piano.
She has two sons and can do the splits.

I would love to be like Sue
because I would like to be flexible
and athletic.
I would like to be musical
but it's a lot of money.
I bet I will be like her.

Molly Symes (9)
Trull 1st Brownies, Taunton

My Mum

Sarah is my mum
Who is a lifeguard.
I look up to her all the time,
My mum wins lots of medals.
Mum, Mum, Mum, she's all I ever think about.
I love everything to do with her.
Now I see how lucky I am to have her.
Gentle, kind and caring she is!

Daisylea Perry (8)
Trull 1st Brownies, Taunton

The Lady With The Lamp - Haiku

Inspired by the war
Went to help men, young and old,
The girl with the lamp.

Truly horrified
At the sight of rats and dirt,
The girl with the lamp.

The doctors said no
But she never gave up, no
The girl with the lamp.

We really need to
Thank her for hospitals now,
The girl with the lamp.

Molly Heath (9)
Trull 1st Brownies, Taunton

Pope John Paul II

Pope John Paul II
Generous
Kind
Caring for the world as Jesus did
Cradling us in his arms.

Hannah Hubbuck (8)
25th Newcastle English Martyrs' Brownie Guide Pack, Fenham

Florence Nightingale

Lovely and generous in every way,
Never stopped working a single day
Regardless of those long damp nights.
She never stopped carrying her lights!

Lady with the lamp.

Molly McCaffrey (9)
25th Newcastle English Martyrs' Brownie Guide Pack, Fenham

Mary Mother Of Jesus

Mary, Mother of Jesus
Helper of life,
Kind and loving.
Thoughtful and caring,
Unhappy when her son Jesus was
Put to death.
Hanging on a cross because
He loved us.

Loryn Davison (8)
25th Newcastle English Martyrs' Brownie Guide Pack, Fenham

Florence Nightingale

A light shining in the darkness
Lighting up the dark cellar.
Healing when no one else could
Dirt, rats and germs, all around her.
She lit up the hospital
Brought hope to the world.

Melia Ewart (9)
25th Newcastle English Martyrs' Brownie Guide Pack, Fenham

Mary

Loving to everyone
Brave when she was all alone
Caring for Jesus
When he needs her
Our Holy Mother.

Courtney Benson (8)
25th Newcastle English Martyrs' Brownie Guide Pack, Fenham

Mary

Brave, travelling far
Giving birth to the Son of God.
Lonely, sad after His death.
Our caring Mother.

Laura Bell (8)
25th Newcastle English Martyrs' Brownie Guide Pack, Fenham

Florence Nightingale

Carrying a lamp,
Smelly, dirty hospitals.
Caring for the sick,
Loving
Bandaging up people.
Looking after soldiers.

Lauren Kenny (9)
25th Newcastle English Martyrs' Brownie Guide Pack, Fenham

The Queen

Thoughtful, caring,
Giving service all her life,
Cares about everyone.
Beautiful palace,
Beautiful clothes,
But a life lived for her people.

Emily Wilkinson (7)
25th Newcastle English Martyrs' Brownie Guide Pack, Fenham

My Mum

My mum rocks
She cleans my socks
She once said to me,
'Be, who you want to be.'
She's funny, foolish
And sometimes coolish.
She makes me food
Even when I'm in a mood.
She loves me for me
That's why she inspires me.

Rebecca Marrs
1st Southbourne Brownies, Southbourne

My Teacher

My favourite teacher is Mr E
He is very special to me,
I wish he was back just to see
If he still remembers me.

This year he has gone
To teach in Hong Kong.
Please come back
I wish and pray
To stay for another day.

Shannon McCormick (9)
1st Southbourne Brownies, Southbourne

Mums

Mums are helpful and kind
Mums are angels
And look like them too
Cool mums are helpful and kind
I love mums because
They give you anything.

Emily Smith (11)
6th Hereford Salvation Army, Hereford

Grandad

Hospital never stopped him,
Bless him, he's still going.
He's a star,
Even though he's had problems with his heart.
He's a bit wealthy
And somewhat healthy,
But even so, I love him lots!

Jessica Annett (11)
6th Hereford Salvation Army, Hereford

My Mum

We always share secrets,
she can see me straight through.
She's always there for me,
in everything I do.

We both love chocolate, we don't know
which ones to pick!
But I will tell you now
we'll both end up feeling *sick!*

There has never been a moment
when we didn't get on!
We will be *best mates forever,*
for as long as the world goes on.

She's one in a million, and I would
just like to say, *'Mum,* you're a *star,*
and I love you that way!'

Claire Arch (13)
4th Bourne Guides, Bourne

My Dance Teacher

I love to dance, leap and prance.
Thanks to my dance teacher.

She is so kind, she has a free mind.
That's my dance teacher.

Modern I dance, my class we all prance.
We're inspired by our dance teacher.

All my friends go to dance
Because they all like to prance.

We all like our dance teacher.

Laura Jones (11)
4th Bourne Guides, Bourne

Friends

Friends are cool
Friends are fab
Friends are exciting
Friends are mad.

My friends are funny
They make me laugh
We play outside
And work in class.

Friends are helpful
When trouble comes
We tell our friends
But not our mums.

When I have a troubled night,
My friends will listen to my dreams.
They share my problems and my thoughts,
Then explain to me what it all means,
When my friends cry, I help them out because
Friends are cool
Friends are fab
Friends are exciting
Friends are mad.

Steph Gostling (13)
4th Bourne Guides, Bourne

Darcie Bussell

Who is Darcie Bussell?
Won't be seen doing the hustle!
She glides with grace,
Hours of her smiley face.
Who is Darcie Bussell?

She dances on the tips of her toes,
Waiting happily in her pose.
Beautiful, happy ballet dancer,
Leaping, balancing, flexible prancer,
She dances on the tips of her toes.

Inspiring people here today,
End of her shows, hear 'Hip hip hooray!'
Free movement, classical, any kind.
All these moves inside her mind,
Inspiring people here today.

Hammond School student
Where she practised her movement
Being what she is today.
Everyone wants to copy her way,
Hammond School student.

Who is Darcie Bussell?
Her speciality isn't hustle,
Our beautiful English fame,
Pictures of her in my frame.
Who is Darcie Bussell?

Molly Pritchard (9)
9th Chester Brownies, Chester

Jamie Maguire

A boy in my class called Jamie Maguire,
He, for me, is the perfect one to inspire.
He can do flips and cartwheels too,
Lots of gymnasts he's similar to.

One-handed handstands and cartwheels,
But first he needs a lot of good meals.
A lot of people he does inspire
That's my friend, Jamie Maguire.

Victoria Hare (10)
9th Chester Brownies, Chester

Auntie Margaret

The person I admire most is kind, brave,
Forgiving and helpful.
She never shouts or gets mad,
She is always there by my side.
The person I admire most is my auntie Margaret.

Stephanie Camy (9)
9th Chester Brownies, Chester

God

God inspires me because He made the Earth and me,
He looks after the poor people and people in the universe.
He has powers that can rule the world.

Hannah Maloney (7)
9th Chester Brownies, Chester

Alex B

I'm inspired by Alex B,
Because she always played with me.
But one sad Christmas Eve,
Her mum closed her eyes and
Now up, up, up she flies, with the angels
In the skies.
So now she plays happily,
With her new family.

Georgina Pritchard (7)
9th Chester Brownies, Chester

J K Rowling

J K Rowling is my star,
Writing and thinking in Scotland afar.
Six amazing books she has written,
All of them I have and I'm smitten

'Harry Potter' is my favourite book,
Imagination, adventure and lots of fun.
From a person's mind, this story begun
Harry, Hermione and Ron - they're chums.

Rebekah Corner (10)
9th Chester Brownies, Chester

Florence Nightingale

Florence did a lot for our soldiers
She made them better and cosy
She kept them well and hopeful
That's Florence Nightingale

Florence did a lot for our hospitals
She made them clean and tidy
She made it a safe place to go
That's Florence Nightingale

Florence did a lot for us
She inspired nurses to help people
She made medicines come a long way
That's Florence Nightingale.

Kirsty Huggins (11)
1st Thorpe Willerby Guides, Selby

Lesley Garrett

I am doing Lesley Garrett because
She is the reason we have our
House at school, she inspired us
She did and very well too.

Our school is very proud of her
Because she' the best and that
Is why I look up to her, I do, I do.

She has such a lovely singing voice
I wish I had one too but
I sound like water going down the loo!

So that's why I look up to her, I do, I do
She's the woman that gave us our
House at school, she's very cool!

Kate Rowbotham (12)
1st Thorpe Willerby Guides, Selby

Thank You!

Sally, Sammy and Jenny
What great people they are.
What wonderful dances they've taught me
Oh how many!
When I would be feeling low,
They could always cheer me up!
I thank you for bringing these
People into the world.

Lucie Baillie (10)
1st Thorpe Willerby Guides, Selby

My Family

F un times happen with my family,

A mber is my family pet dog

M ummy and daddy sometimes take me out to play

I love to play with my brother William

Y es, love to all my family.

Charlotte Balls (8)
3rd Oulton Brownies, Lowestoft

My Cats

I have two little cats
Their coats are so warm
If I don't hurt them
They will do me no harm.

They stay in my house
Nearly all day
When I get home from school,
They then want to play.

Lady and Tiny welcome me home
In their own little way
A miaow from them both
Really brightens my day.

Laura Gibson (9)
3rd Oulton Brownies, Lowestoft

My Home, I Love It

M y home is my favourite place in the world
Y ou have a home too?

H appy in my own home
O ur own home
M y big house and what it is
E verywhere I go, I feel warm

I love my home

L ittle things made a big difference
O ut of the door into the garden
V ery big, my house is
E very day I wake up in my bed

I don't want to leave my house
T ime goes by, in my house.

Elise Reid (9)
3rd Oulton Brownies, Lowestoft

My Nan

I looked up to my nan
I was her biggest fan
She always has a smile for me
Especially when I went round for tea.

The games we played together
Will be something I'll always treasure
If I needed to talk, she was there
Her love was always there to share.

Her kind and loving way
She always had a good word to say.
I don't need to have any fame,
To be like her is my aim.

Now we are apart
She is always in my heart.

Bethany Lark (9)
3rd Oulton Brownies, Lowestoft

My Big Bad Bro

If anybody knows me
as well as he
you would know
that I wouldn't say
this about him . . .

He cheers me up
when I am down
He's helped me with
my maths
I've improved in
leaps and bounds.

He sticks up for me
when I am bullied.
He comforts me
when I am alone.

I know this sounds
weird to my friends
but he *is* my bro and
I love him.

He is annoying nearly
all the time.
He can be scary too,
he's my big bad bro!

Imogen James (11)
1st Wribbenhall Guides, Wribbenhall

My Mum

My mum is the best
she always helps me with
my homework and when
I am good, I get a treat.

She takes me to the cinema
and takes me to lots of cool places.
She is the best!

Coral Herbert (11)
1st Wribbenhall Guides, Wribbenhall

My Inspiration - Oak Tree

By the Golden Valley she stands alone,
Mice scuttle by to their home.
She's stood for more than twenty years,
Though no marks of age she bears.
Orange leaves in autumn and her peeling bark,
Until the summer brings a singing lark.
Her great big branches reach
And lovely flowers spread.
Though as the winter comes,
Everything seems dead.

Jessica Stuart-Smith (13)
1st Wribbenhall Guides, Wribbenhall

My Mum

Mum is my chum
although she smacks my bum,
Mum is the greatest.
Out of her and dad, she lets me stay up the latest.

She is the kindest mum ever
she's smart and very clever.
Mum helps me with homework
(she showed me how the phone works).

Cookery, maths, reading,
she knows it all.
She even helped me in PE
to climb up a rock cave wall.

She takes me to the doctors,
she takes me to the dentist.
She's a unique mum, there's
not another one like my mum.

Mum is sweet, mum is cuddly,
but when it comes to food,
gosh, she's fussy!

She sorts out my problems,
she sorts out my fears and
she wipes away my tears.

Ciara Mole (9)
2nd Baldock Brownies, Baldock

Nanny

Nanny always gives me lots and lots of nice presents.
I always look up to her whenever I feel sad and unhappy.
My nanny gives me someone to talk to, I get to stay round for the night
And she lets me get sweets from the corner shop.
I love you nanny, you are the best.
You are better than all the *rest!*

Alana Sullivan (7)
2nd Baldock Brownies, Baldock

Untitled

About my mum . . .
My mum is special
My mum is sweet,
Even though she tells me off.
I love my mum, I let her rest.
I love you Mum, you're the best.

Tilly Doherty (7)
2nd Baldock Brownies, Baldock

Untitled

I want to be a singer, I learn every hit by heart
My heroes are the clever girls who make it in the charts.

But when I'm rich and famous, I won't forget my pack
I'll send them all a photo of me and I'll sign it on the back.

You can stay at my penthouse apartment, or visit my yacht in the Med
You can camp in my Surrey acres or stay in the guest suite instead.

It may never happen but I'm going to give it a go,
And one day my dream may come true
You just never, never know!

Megan Griffiths (11)
3rd Kenley (All Saints) Guides, Kenley

My Nominee

Chonika is like a rose that opens like a flower,
you can always approach her because she shows
me much love.

She's caring and understanding
and helps me loads,

That's why I nominate Chonika,
because she's like a rose.

You can ask her as a Guider,
what ideas can I do?
She'll share and point you in the right direction,
that there's a lot you can do.

She's funny and she's strict sometimes,
but I don't mind at all, because she's showing me responsibility
that I can be someone who's proud and tall.

You inspire and guide me,
I hope you win this mate!
You go ahead Chonika and be the candidate.

Jenine Chue (11)
3rd Sudbury Guides, Middlesex

Michael Morpurgo

You're like a light in the fridge - always on,
Your books are always great, but never wrong.

I think to write books, you have to be clever,
So please keep writing books for ever and ever.

Your books are different in colour and size,
Opening and reading a new one, has its own surprise.

Michael, your books can be about anything you choose,
I hope that one day I can be in your shoes.

I think to write books, you have to be clever,
So please keep writing books, for ever and ever.

Jessica Button (11)
1st St Breward Guide Unit, Bodmin

A Brownie

A Brownie I am
A Brownie I'll be
Until I'm a Guide
Then no Brownies for me.

But just for now
A Brownie I'll be
And be happy to help
When someone asks me.

I could be a dancer
But - a Brownie I'll be
I try to be good, kind
And gentle, you see.

A lot you can learn
So a Brownie I'll be
My leaders - Brown Owl and Snowy
Teach me a lot, you see.

In my Brownie uniform
A Brownie I'll be
And be glad that I am
Because, I know it's me!

Courtney Healy (10)
282nd Glasgow Brownies, Glasgow

My Best Friend

My best friend is happy and jolly
She is kind and helpful
She helps me with everything I do
She plays with me when I am left out
I think she is my best friend
Don't you?

Annabelle Lee (7)
2nd Newton Brownies, West Kirby

My Friend

I have a friend called Anabelle Lee
and she has come to my house for tea.
She is my friend and she can bend,
Anabelle is very nice and
she will fetch a high price.

Anabelle's writing is very neat
and she can touch her head with her feet.
Anabelle is one year younger and
she didn't like it when a bee stung her!

Anabelle is my Brownie buddy,
we have good fun and sometimes get muddy.

Hannah Corless (8)
2nd Newton Brownies, West Kirby

My Dad

My dad likes to snore
When he stops he does some more.
When he snores, he sounds like a rooster,
I think that is how he got his nickname - Brookster!
My dad has lots of friends from north to south
And east to west.
The trouble is, in work he is the best.

Kirsty Brooks (10)
1st Ard Jiass Guides, Isle of Man

Kelly Clarkson

She went on American Idol
And ended up winning the votes.
She went on to be famous
As a singer, with talented coats.

Her voice can heal all pains,
She sings like a beautiful dove.
Her heart is full of goodness,
Full of warmth and love.

Her face is full of sparkle,
Her eyes glisten like a light,
Beautiful thoughts fulfil her,
She's full of strength and might.

This is why I love her,
She's my favourite star.
I hope she will continue,
I hope she can go far.

Megan Faragher (12)
1st Ard Jiass Guides, Isle of Man

My Inspiration

Miss Chapman my English teacher
has many amazing features!

She brightens up the class
and makes us all laugh.

Once we arrive in the room,
the lesson ends all too soon.

Then I hand in my book,
not believing my luck,
to have such a great teacher!

Heather Booth (12)
1st Ard Jiass Guides, Isle of Man

Inspiration

Faye White is my inspiration
She has lots of dedication
She kicks the ball like David Beckham
But doesn't get his recognition
She runs round the pitch like Superman
All the time looking very glam
She has lots of skill with the ball
And will never let her team fall.

Hannah Leece (12)
1st Ard Jiass Guides, Isle of Man

Elvis Presley

His groovy music lifted the roof,
His hair was black with a slight poof.
His title was The King of Rock,
But later in life, he ran amok.
Like no other man, he shook his hips,
And caused the girls to scream and skip.
His death was caused by junk food,
But still in life he's called a dude.
His music made the whole world scream,
'Your music is by far supreme!'
All money flew into his hands
And by far he could defeat all bands.
He is my hero of all fame,
Elvis Presley, that's his name!

Kelly Firth (11)
1st Ard Jiass Guides, Isle of Man

Proud

Kelly Holmes:

Every step closer, every step near,
running without any fear,
She runs for victory, she runs for joy,
faster than any living boy.
Appreciating any thing
even when she's in the ring.
Gliding along the thin, thin ice,
making sure she doesn't slice.
Winning all the races,
even in different places.
Running for her home,
dodging all the cones.

Abigail Swayne (11)
1st Ard Jiass Guides, Isle of Man

My Mom

My mom inspires me
she's very funny,
She sings songs all the time
and she gives me lots of money.
My mom inspires me, she's very sweet,
she calls me Honey and makes
good things to eat.
My mom loves me
I love her too,
Without my mum
my life would be poo!

Ashley Pilling (11)
1st Ard Jiass Guides, Isle of Man

Lance Armstrong

Wow! What a smashing guy.
The year he thought he would lose it,
The year he thought he would die.
But eventually he conquered it,
He won the Tour de France.
He isn't good at singing,
He isn't good at dance,
But he's fantastic on a bike.
He overcame his cancer.
Wow! What a smashing guy.

Heather Murray (12)
1st Ard Jiass Guides, Isle of Man

Kelly Holmes

An inspiration is Kelly Holmes,
you will never hear any moans.
Through the bad times
she's made by miles.
Suffered from depression
give that consideration.
She beat it though.
how could anyone say so - she's a star.
She will get so far
an inspiration is Kelly Holmes.
That's you told, so
tell a friend of her wonders
and forget those little blunders.

Martha Manini (12)
1st Ard Jiass Guides, Isle of Man

Jacqueline Wilson

This best-selling author is so cool,
When she is writing, she totally rules!
Her books draw me in, and I can't get away,
They are so inspirational,
I could read them all day.
She has many fans across the UK,
Who buy each of her books and don't care
What they pay.
I can assure you though, they get their money's worth,
I can also assure you, she's the best author on Earth.

Jade Booth (10)
1st Ard Jiass Guides, Isle of Man

RE

M r Wright is ace,
R eal in every case.

W ould he teach PE?
R ocking he would be.
I f he went to another school,
G oing, would be very cruel.
H e would have to stay
T o please us in every way.

Léa Bazille (12)
1st Ard Jiass Guides, Isle of Man

My Family

M is for marvellous mummy
Y is for the yummy dinners my mum cooks for me

F is for my fabulous father
A is for my adult brother who thinks he is an adult, but he isn't
M is for mad Mum who shouts a lot
I is for illnesses, my mum protects me from
L is for loving and caring all the time
Y is for my yelling brother who yells like my mum.

Lucy Barlow (11)
1st Ard Jiass Guides, Isle of Man

My Nanna

Nanna is the best in the world,
and she is always with me
Never apart, we are the best team
even when I'm sad, she is there.
She is a ray of sunlight always on me.
No one can take her place!

Natalie Davies (10)
3rd Aberdare Brownies, Aberdare

My Best Mum

My mum is the best mum ever
She looks after me every day
I think she should be a queen one day
She helps me with my homework
My mum makes the best food ever
I really want to be her - one day
To be a good mother just like her.

Megan Glover (8)
3rd Aberdare Brownies, Aberdare

Jeremy

Jeremy is good.
I should practise, oh I should.
I wish I could play like him,
One day I could.
He can be catchy, oh yes he can!

He is smart,
He doesn't do art
Homework he can't mark.

Jennie Williams (8)
3rd Aberdare Brownies, Aberdare

My Friend

A my is my best friend
M uch she cares for me
Y ou would love to meet her

J oking and playing
O h so fun
N o stopping us now
E very day we like to play in the burning
S un.

Emily Murphy (9)
3rd Aberdare Brownies, Aberdare

Mother

M other is the closest thing I have had, she is always there for me.

O ther times she shouts at me but it teaches me a lesson.

T he times I am sad she will come and comfort me.

H er hair is blacky brown.

E very time we like our play, as long as we are good.

R eady for a day to end and end with a prayer.

Joanne Hancock (8)
3rd Aberdare Brownies, Aberdare

My Mam

M y mam cooks my food
Y our mam could be like my mum

M y mam makes my bed
A mam like mine is the best
M y mam loves me
 I love my mam.

Mellissa Watkins (7)
3rd Aberdare Brownies, Aberdare

Mother's Day

M y mum is so nice.

O h she loves me oh so much.

T he time I wake up I want to give her a hug.

H er cool jazz she sings to me.

E very day she does something for me.

R eally good she is to me.

S ometimes I get lonely and she cheers me up.

D ays and days of love she gives.

A nd all I want to say is thank you.

Y ou really want to meet her, she is really nice.

Kate Scorey (10)
3rd Aberdare Brownies, Aberdare

My Dad

My dad is the best in the world!
He tickles me and makes me laugh!
He is really cool!
No one would be better than my *dad!*

Megan Hughes (8)
3rd Aberdare Brownies, Aberdare

Mother's Day

M y mum is the best ever,
O n some days she is kind,
T he other days she is not,
H er hair is blonde, her eyes are blue,
E very day she is kind,
R ough at times,
S o kind I love her,

D ays go by, she loves me even more,
A mum like mine is the best,
Y es, I love my mum!

Hannah Jones (9)
3rd Aberdare Brownies, Aberdare

My Mammy

My mammy is the best person in the world
She is very kind and lovely.
I love my mammy so much.
My mother tells me to be careful
When I use sharp stuff.
My mum makes really nice food and meals.
If I ask to go somewhere she lets me go
But I need to go with her.

Georgia Meredith (7)
3rd Aberdare Brownies, Aberdare

My Best Friend Aimee

A imee is very caring, she is my best friend
I want to be her one day
M aybe she will be a star someday
E very time I see her she puts a smile on my face
E very time I think of her I always want to be her more.

Megan Edey (9)
3rd Aberdare Brownies, Aberdare

Mammy

M y mother is sweet, my mother is the best
A nd she is cuddly
M y mother is so kind she buys me treats on Sunday
M y mother takes me places where I want to go
Y our dreams will come true when your mother is by you.

Rachel Hancock (8)
3rd Aberdare Brownies, Aberdare

My Mother

M y mother is so kind,
Y ou would want to meet her.

M akes my bed, cooks my food, irons my clothes
O h yes she does
T ime after time, always helping out
H er lovely cooking I eat every day.
E very second of the day I think about her.
R eady to wrap me up with love.

Amy Jones (10)
3rd Aberdare Brownies, Aberdare

Mother

My mother is the best thing that ever happened to me.
She always buys me things and takes me where I want to go.
And I also have chocolate like a caramel Freddo.
When I am naughty she always comes up to me
And says for once I'll set you free.
And when I'm sad and lonely she always teases me
And once she said come and do the dishes
Or you will go to bed!

Rhiannon Fear (9)
3rd Aberdare Brownies, Aberdare

My Best Friend Bethan

B ethan has put excitement into my life,
E ven when we both go off in moods,
T he funny thing is, we make up in seconds,
H er hair is brown, her eyes are blue
A nd she is my best friend,
N obody's as good as Bethan!

Lauren Kerr (10)
3rd Aberdare Brownies, Aberdare

Brown Owl

Brown Owl is great
She's my best mate.

Her big Brownie smile
Goes on for a mile.

She is always very busy
And never gets in a tizzy.

She's great at craft, games and fun
It doesn't matter if there's no sun.

Pack holiday she will take us
And never shouts if we make a fuss.

We love you Brown Owl
Thank you, thank you, thank you.

Kimberlee Davies (8)
3rd Aberdare Brownies, Aberdare

I Love You

You motivate me just to get through the day
I think about you when I'm feeling down
Because thinking of you never fails to make me laugh and smile.

Whilst in your company I feel safe;
I feel free to be myself and know you accept me for who I am.

I look forward to spending time with you
Your amazing ability to make me laugh until my stomach aches
Is addictive and I never get bored of us laughing together.

You are always there to talk and listen
But never talk down to me; I feel as though I can tell you everything.

Your amazing sense of humour and enjoyment for life
Inspires me to be like you in the future.
Your loving, patient, understanding, caring, mad, fun,
Positive, hardworking, warm, approachable character
Brightens even the dullest days.

Life would be so much more pleasant if everyone was like you;
But if everyone was the same; you wouldn't be so special.

I thank you for just being you and for allowing me to just be me
And I look forward to many more happy memories together.

You are my inspiration, my motivation and I love you.

Helen Watret (15)
11th Loughborough Guides, Loughborough

Friend

F un can be lots of different things for everyone around,
R ain and wind can put you down but Sophie and Nikita are friends
forever whatever, we will always be around,
I n the dead of the night when you fall over we will always
be around to help,
E veryone around knows that we are friends
and we're around somewhere.
N ever let your sadness get you down.
D on't let your school work stop you from making friends,
Sophie and Nikita will always be around to help you
make friends with everyone.

Nikita Thompson & Sophie Bond (11)
11th Loughborough Guides, Loughborough

You're My Everything

I look up to you, for everything you do,
You just lay back and be what you want to be,
And doing what you want to,
I live in a world full of nightmares and bad dreams,
But you inspired me to be what I want to be,
You told me to be me,
And not what they want me to be,
You showed me how to be a sinner, a saint
And how to enjoy every day
And this is why you're my everything,
And my best mate.

Tammy McNeill (15)
11th Loughborough Guides, Loughborough

My Nana

I miss my nana
I miss her cuddle
She made me laugh
All the time
Photographs remind me
Of that time
But most of all I love her
Very, very much
Although she has gone to Heaven.

Eilish Robinson (9)
2nd Chapel Allerton Brownies, Leeds

My Best Mate Rebecca

Rebecca is my best, best friend,
I hope our friendship never ends,
She comes to my house quite a lot,
Both of us tend to lose the plot
But at the end of a long, long day,
I can turn around and easily say,
I've picked her from many others -
I must say, she's better than my brothers.

Beth Kay (9)
2nd Chapel Allerton Brownies, Leeds

Grandad

G randad made me laugh he is the only grandad I had
   but sad to say he died when I was 3.

R ed roses were Grandad's favourite flowers.

A t night, before I go to bed he called me Chubby Cheeks.

N erves he had before he got on stage.

D ad used to call him dad.

A very kind person he was indeed,
   he's the only grandad you could wish for.

D ad is the best person in my life.

Saskia McBride (9)
2nd Chapel Allerton Brownies, Leeds

Jemima

J emima's nickname is 'Mima'
E stands for energetic
M arvellous girl
I ndependent and pretty girl
M agnificent
A mazing friend.

Louise Fahy (9)
2nd Chapel Allerton Brownies, Leeds

My Florence Nightingale

F lorence Nightingale was a nurse

L iked to look after people

O ver the Crimean War she looked after soldiers

R eading books and learning about nursing.

E very day she looked after her patients.

N ever was mean.

C aring for her patients.

E very morning she checked up on her patients.

Eimear Lynch (9)
2nd Chapel Allerton Brownies, Leeds

Granbob

G reat man
R eliable
A lways there
N ose broken
B orn in Sunderland
O ur grandad
B est friend.

Catherine Iles (9)
2nd Chapel Allerton Brownies, Leeds

My Brownie Poem

B eing kind to everyone
R especting the leaders
O bey the Brownie Guide Law
W earing the correct uniform
N ew friends
I nviting visitors
E njoying different activities
S mile to everyone around.

Shannon Doherty (9)
2nd Chapel Allerton Brownies, Leeds

My Best Friend - Beth

I know she can be annoying,
I know she's rather mad,
But she brightens my day,
In every way
And she's the best friend I've ever had.

Beth is a friend from outer space,
She can bring a grin to my face
And I know that her smile
Lasts for a mile,
But she's the best friend I've ever had.

Rebecca O'Reilly (10)
2nd Chapel Allerton Brownies, Leeds

Catherine

C atherine is my best friend.

A nd always plays with me.

T he best thing about her is that she is funny.

H er sister is funny like her.

E very day I look forward to seeing her.

R is for a good runner 'cause she is one.

I always have fun with her.

N ever do we fall out.

E very time we play together we play fun games.

Laura Jordens-Harris (8)
2nd Chapel Allerton Brownies, Leeds

Emily

E mily is very funny and smiley

M is for magical

I is for incredible because I think she is incredible.

L is for lovely because she lets me have some of her crisps.

Y ou are my best friend Emily.

Dana Llewellyn (8)
2nd Chapel Allerton Brownies, Leeds

Annabel

A nnabel is my best friend
N ever does she tell lies
N ice is for Annabel
A nd she always has the giggles,
B eautiful is Annabel
E xciting things me and Annabel do
L is for love Annabel shares.

Jessica Maruniak (8)
2nd Chapel Allerton Brownies, Leeds

My Best Friend Jessica

My friend is kind and friendly
She is funny and laughs at me.
She is a little bit annoying and asks me questions.
I have fall outs with her sometimes
But then we say sorry and make friends
And she is brilliant.

Annabel Uttley (8)
2nd Chapel Allerton Brownies, Leeds

Dana

D ana is my best friend
A nd she always has the giggles
N ice girl is she
A nd never makes me upset.

Emily Uttley (8)
2nd Chapel Allerton Brownies, Leeds

Elizabeth

E is for exciting because she is exciting.

L is for laughing because she makes me laugh.

I is for I always look forward to seeing her.

Z is for zany as a galloping zebra

A nd she always gets the giggles.

B is for the pretty bluebells because she looks like one.

E is for Elizabeth because that's her name.

T is for she's always talking to me when I am upset.

H is for happy because she is always happy.

Mary Iles (8)
2nd Chapel Allerton Brownies, Leeds

My Sister

My sister always laughs,
My sister always smiles,
I think she is the best one of all.

My sister always giggles,
My sister always sniffles,
My sister has the cold,
That's why she always dribbles.

My sister always cuddles me
To show that she loves me,
But best of all my sister always
Kisses me and gives me rosy cheeks.

Samantha Boyle (12)
75th Dundee Rainbows, Dundee

My Guiding Light

I have got a mum
Who is always fun.
She does great things for me
Like making my tea.

She has curly hair
And she is very fair.
She might not be in a magazine
But I think she's as beautiful as a queen.

Shelley Mulholland (10)
9th Withington Brownies, Manchester

My Special Friend

A special friend is someone
Who picks me up when I am down,
Makes me smile when I frown,
Calms me down when I am mad,
Lends me an ear when I am sad.

A special friend is always true
So thank you for just being you.

Shannon Corr (10)
9th Withington Brownies, Manchester

The Budgie Who Inspires Me

My budgie's bewitching beauty
Inspired me to call him Cutie.
His golden feathers dazzle in the sun,
And dinging his bell is what he calls fun.

His eyes are onyx black,
His breast is emerald green,
He twinkles like a star,
His radiant plumage gleams.

He is caring as the sun,
He is wise as the moon.
He is light as a feather,
And I hope to see him soon.

Alusia Malinowska (10)
9th Withington Brownies, Manchester

My Family

My family
My family
They are the best
I do the dishes
And they do the rest
But it is lucky that they get to bed
But after that they get up
And get me fed.

Megan Clapperton (8)
1st Linnvale Brownies, Linnvale

My Family

This is my family 1, 2, 3
There's Mum, Dad, Scott and me!
There's my gran who always invites us for tea
And Grandpa who sits me on his knee.
This is my family 1, 2, 3
There's Mum, Dad, Scott and . . . *me!*

Emma Fulton (10)
1st Linnvale Brownies, Linnvale

Brownie Friend

If you are a Brownie friend,
The fun never ends!
We sing songs and play games
And sometimes we make picture frames.
Donna, Sally, Linda, Stacy and Nancy,
Aren't their names fancy?
The moles, the rabbits and the hedgehogs,
Some people wanted the dogs!
We love Brownies,
Yes it's true,
Why don't you come and join in too?

Amy-Leigh Quantick (10)
1st Linnvale Brownies, Linnvale

School

Schools are loud, messy and fun,
When it's break we lay in the sun.
Mucking around all day long
And in assembly we would have a good sing-song.
My favourite lesson is art,
My friends help me and they are really smart.

Home time is the best,
Because we can go home and have a rest.
Doing homework for most of the night,
Waking up in the morning when it's bright.
Ready to start another day,
When we will go out and play.

Teachers screaming and shouting,
Telling us what to do.
My favourite teacher is Mr Gurr,
But we have to call him sir.
You can always see him at the pub,
At school he runs an English club.

Ellie Smith (13)
1st Lenham Guides, Maidstone

I Love My Mummy

I love you Mummy
You are pretty when it is sunny
You smile in the rain
Even though it is a pain
In spring you are happy
When I was a baby you changed my nappy
You help me with my homework
You do all the work
You love me
And you laugh with glee
You take me to school
You even try to know with wool
At night when I am scared
You let me into your bed
Your poor old head
I love you Mummy.

Abbie Neal (7)
5th Tooting St Boniface Brownies, Tooting

Craig Tanner - The Football Player

When I go to watch football,
He always stands tall.
He's the captain of my favourite team,
His name is Craig Tanner.
He has such a nice manner.
He is caring and never is mean.
I got his autograph
As he walks down the path
He smiled and waved at me.
When I watch the game
It's never the same
His inspiration is clear to see.

Anna Creegan (10)
5th Tooting St Boniface Brownies, Tooting

God Inspires Me

The person who inspires me is God,
He makes the sea flow for the cod.
He loves everyone including sinners
He's not racist, if we're fat or thinner.
God makes the Earth and Heaven
On Earth there are places like Devon.
God is the Lord and King,
He is the Lord who made everything.
Lord loves us and we love Him,
For many things.

Catriona Cormack (9)
5th Tooting St Boniface Brownies, Tooting

Mr Kendall

Mr Kendall is very funny,
He dips his bread in honey.

He likes to write,
All about insects that bite.

Mr Kendall has lots of expressions
But has nothing to say in confession.

Clara Hernon (8)
5th Tooting St Boniface Brownies, Tooting

My Grandad

He's as sweet as honey,
He's as kind as a flower,
My grandad, my grandad,
He is caring and helpful,
He is never rude or mean,
My grandad, my grandad,
He loves football,
He never misses a match,
My grandad, my grandad,
He is such a bookworm
And so am I,
His inspiration is clear to see,
My grandad, my grandad!

Danielle Sams (9)
5th Tooting St Boniface Brownies, Tooting

My Friend Lizzie

My friend Lizzie is very funny,
She is sweet like the bees' honey.
She's very kind,
But sometimes out of her mind.
She's got a silly giggle
And likes to wiggle.
She's very good at gymnastics
And doesn't lose very many incentive ticks.
She does loads of flips
But never slips.
She does very hilarious things,
But she hardly ever sings.
She always cheers me up
And congratulated me
When I won the poetry cup.
She can do lots of cool voices,
But doesn't like tortoises.
She is very funky
And her favourite animal is a monkey.
My friend Lizzie is very funny.

Ekaete Bassey (9)
5th Tooting St Boniface Brownies, Tooting

Minette

My sister Minette is very kind
She's always looking for something to find,
She plays the piano and helps me at home
Which stops my mum having a moan.

My sister Minette is my favourite sister
Always finding a plaster for my nasty blister
She helps with my homework and housework at home
My sister Minette, she never does moan!

Georgia Paes (9)
5th Tooting St Boniface Brownies, Tooting

Beyoncé

My poem is about Beyoncé
She dresses in a cool way,
Her voice is so great,
I'd love to be her mate.
I think she's very pretty
And she lives in the city.

Jessica Owusu-Bekoe (9)
5th Tooting St Boniface Brownies, Tooting

My Mummy

I love my mummy
She's really sweet, sweeter than honey.
My mummy always makes my dinner,
So I know I won't get any thinner.
In the daytime she brushes my hair
And at bedtime she kisses me and my bear.
She always does my homework with me
And if I get it right, I jump with glee
She brings me to school
And when I come home she asks me, 'Did you fall?'
She loves me very much
And I cuddle her with a gentle touch.
At bedtime my mummy kisses me and says goodnight
And she helps me when I have a fright.

Kathleen Ryan (7)
5th Tooting St Boniface Brownies, Tooting

My Mother

My mother is the best thing on Earth,
I've liked her since she gave birth.
She is an excellent cook
And loves to read books,
For I could never name all the things she's worth.

Lizzie Hay (9)
5th Tooting St Boniface Brownies, Tooting

Miss Reegan

Miss Reegan is so kind and gentle,
Even though her class is mental.
She gives them sweets and lots of treats
And does enjoy all kinds of meats.
She does like sprouts, but never shouts,
When she is fishing she catches trouts.

Laura Akehurst (9)
5th Tooting St Boniface Brownies, Tooting

Mrs Kerins

My head teacher is Mrs Kerins
And I know for sure her favourite sauce is Lea and Perrins.
Her voice is lovely, her singing is great,
She certainly inspires me never to be late,
She always smiles and never runs a mile.

Madeleine Hay (8)
5th Tooting St Boniface Brownies, Tooting

My Friend Inspires Me

My friend is funny,
My friend is kind,
My friend is caring,
We get along together just fine,
She is always there for me.

Megan Nassé (8)
5th Tooting St Boniface Brownies, Tooting

My Ballet Teacher

My ballet teacher inspires me,
I go to her lessons after tea.
She's ever so kind,
If we mess about she doesn't mind.
Her long, brown hair is in a bun,
She's so much fun.
She can do the splits,
When I'm with her I never fall in my cross pit.
My ballet teacher.

Nishoba Kugarajah (8)
5th Tooting St Boniface Brownies, Tooting

Florence Nightingale

Florence Nightingale is a wonderful nurse
Many people fell under her curse.
But the curse is not wicked and evil
It makes you feel like you're in God's cathedral.
She sees cuts and bruises everywhere
But she is always there to care.
Her wonderful talents are clear to see,
She is the one who inspires me!

Tara Nassé (9)
5th Tooting St Boniface Brownies, Tooting

Bernie Coyle

My cousin Bernie inspires me the most;
She the best person in the world
Her pets are so cool!
I love her so much, my cousin Bernie!
She worked for Mountain Rescue,
Her life's amazing,
I love her the best.

I love *Bernie!*

Sian Gillespie (9)
5th Tooting St Boniface Brownies, Tooting

J K Rowling

J oanne Rowling writes my favourite books.

K nowing when I look at them, they are exciting.

R eading her books is my hobby,
O n my reading shelf her books will go,
W riting is the thing she does best,
L ying in bed, thinking for inspirations,
I n time her books are published,
N ever tiring to stop writing,
G oing on for she's my favourite author.

Aislinn Harkin (9)
5th Tooting St Boniface Brownies, Tooting

Well Done!

Well done! Lord and Lady BP!
They knew it was the place to be.
Almost one hundred years ago,
They were the people in the know.
They began this great big game,
Enriched our lives, time and time again.
With honour, friendship and pride,
We all stand together side by side.
A common standard, Guides and Scouts,
But Girl Guiding is what we're all about!

Girls laughing and having fun,
Singing taps, day is done.
Patrol outings, cooking and craft
Fashion shows and acting daft.
Learning about things affecting our world,
Opportunities for each and every girl.
A haunted house sleepover, a summer camp,
Brilliant sunshine, cold, wet and damp!
Whatever the weather, whatever the times
Girl Guiding suits me just fine!

So now I've told you of the things we do,
Does it really appeal to you?
Of the iceberg this is just the tip,
I've only told you a little bit.
The list goes on, it never ends,
Join us now and make new friends.
You can try all these things, and much, much more,
So take that step, open that door!
Try something new, don't be scared,
As a Guide you will always 'be prepared'!

Jessica Goodman (11)
Southbourne Guides, Southbourne

Guides - Cinquain

Guiding
Guiding I love
Fund-raising and outings
But best of all meeting new friends
Love it.

Maddie Lammas (11)
Southbourne Guides, Southbourne

Guiding Gliding

Guiding is memorable
Gliding is like a breath of fresh air
Guiding is respectful
Gliding is free and open, always fair
Guiding is enjoyable
Gliding is a view over the environment
Guiding is about doing your best
Gliding is loving your God
Guiding is helping others
Gliding is looking over your Queen and country.

Rachel Miller (13)
Southbourne Guides, Southbourne

At First

First came Mr Baden-Powell,
Then there was his Mrs,
Next came Boy Scouts bold and proud
But girls knew what they were missing.

His sister Agnes rushed to help,
They formed the Girl Guide movement,
From India the name did come,
For the girls who were pioneering.

Finally his wife Olave,
Became the first chief Guide
And since the start of our great feat,
Our cause has gone world-wide.

Rachel Eberle (13)
Southbourne Guides, Southbourne

Untitled

Guides is cool
We go every Tuesday after school
It's fun to be a Guide,
With all your friends by your side.
Listening to a Barbie song,
Fun to sing along.
We work for badges and raising money
Being a Guide is very funny.

Jennifer Meads (14)
Southbourne Guides, Southbourne

If

If there was no Robert Baden-Powell
  all us Guides would be sitting around.
If there was no Olave Baden-Powell
  all us Guides would be standing around.
If there was no Agnes Baden-Powell
  all us Guides would be lying around.
If there were no Baden-Powells
  there would be no Guides around the world.

Maisie Marshall (12)
Southbourne Guides, Southbourne

Guides Is Cool

Guides is cool,
Guides does rule,
It rocks my world,
Just like cream curled,
We all join in
And we will win,
The best Guide group,
In the world.

Candi Gilroy (13)
Southbourne Guides, Southbourne

Mum

I looked around for inspiration
I looked around for hope
I looked around for something odd
And found it in you

I looked around for something new
I looked around for help
I looked around for those kind acts
And found it in you

I looked around for encouragement
I looked around for praise
I looked around for care and love
And found it in you

I looked around for laughter
I looked around for fun
I looked around for hugs and smiles
And found it in you

I looked around for family
I looked around for sharing
I looked around for that kind face
And found it in you

You are the one who makes it real
You are the one true best
You are the one I love most
Dearest, darling Mum.

Hayley Jones (12)
7th Appleton Guides, Warrington

My Inspiration

Jacqueline Wilson is my leader in books
She leads me all the way

I went to get her autograph, it was a dream come true
I think she's great and wonderful
She makes reading fun and enjoyable
I think her books are good

I read as much as I could
I have read nearly all her books
My best one is 'Candyfloss'
She is my inspiration.

Eleanor Ross (8)
9th Catisfield East Brownies

Just Jodie

Jodie is brill and brings sunshine
Jodie is nice as all things fine
Jodie is great and so kind
And if I lost something she would always find.

Abigail Price (9)
4th Kingswinford Brownies, Kingswinford

My Friend Brittany

My friend Brittany has long hair
She always makes it fair
She never tells me I'm wrong
I have to close my ears
When she sings a song.

Charlotte James (9)
4th Kingswinford Brownies, Kingswinford

Just Grace

I would like to be Grace,
She is both kind and helpful,
She also cheers me up
When I am feeling dreadful
But she also helps other people
When they are feeling blue.
The best is that she is a true friend.
You can't forget that one fact . . .
She is *funny!*

Emma McQuaide (8)
4th Kingswinford Brownies, Kingswinford

Anastasia

Anastasia has a wonderful voice
That sings out loud.
Her voice is so powerful
That it makes the whole world shatter.
She smells of lovely flowers
Her hair is lovely and blonde
I wish I could be her.

Jodie Baker (9)
4th Kingswinford Brownies, Kingswinford

Abbi

Abbi has magical powers
And smells like fresh flowers
She is kind and beautiful
She has a huge smile
Abbi is great at friendships
And she never cries.

Victoria Sidaway (9)
4th Kingswinford Brownies, Kingswinford

Emma

I'd like to be Emma,
She's nice and quiet,
She is a clever helping hand,
She makes me laugh,
She cheers me up,
But most of all,
I have her as a great friend.

Grace Jones (8)
4th Kingswinford Brownies, Kingswinford

Dad

I wish I could be like my dad,
Tall and sensible,
Work for a lot of money,
Dad,
I find,
Is a good friend to me,
Dad,
Is gentle and loving,
Kind,
As well,
I like it,
Instead
Of being miserable,
He's a . . .
Star!

Elizabeth Bowater (7)
4th Kingswinford Brownies, Kingswinford

My Dream

I wish I could be a jockey,
I promise I wouldn't be cocky,
I'd feel free in the air,
And ride on a mare.
My horse would fill the dirty track,
And when I want her to go faster
I would give her a smack.
I would love to win the Royal Cup
And get the others to clean up my pony's muck!
I would love to have roses,
Put on my pony.

Jemima Cooper (9)
4th Kingswinford Brownies, Kingswinford

I Want To Be Kylie

I want to be like Kylie,
Oh yes Kylie.
I want to be a singer
And sing super songs.
I want to wear some make-up
And have an agent.
I would like to wear the clothes she wears
And have lots of fans!

Leah Pearson (7)
4th Kingswinford Brownies, Kingswinford

The Artist

I wish I was an artist
An artist that could draw,
An artist that could draw the sunset high above the sky.
I want to be an artist that can draw the fluffy clouds
Right down into the sea.

Kathryn Wright (8)
4th Kingswinford Brownies, Kingswinford

Flexy Lexie

I look up to Lexie
Because she is so flexy.

She is great at headstands,
The perfect bits are the lands.

Handstands, cartwheels, backflips and rolls
With her dolls
And that is why we call her Flexy Lexie.

Charlotte Oliver (9)
4th Kingswinford Brownies, Kingswinford

Writers - My Inspiration

Books are my inspiration
They make me feel apprehensive
Books take me to another world
Where I am in my own adventure
They inspire me to write and draw
As well as sing and dance
Do they do the same to you?

Naomi Robinson (9)
3rd South Ashford Brownies, Ashford

Mum

My mum is the best,
I love her so much,
She's better than the rest,
I love her touch.

April Oliver (10)
1st Portslade (St Andrews) Brownies

My Dad

My dad cares for me,
We love each other,
Hopefully we will always see each other,
He's the best dad in the world,
I don't know what to say
But my dad loves me every day.

Skye Hobden (9)
1st Portslade (St Andrews) Brownies

My Special Mum

I love my lovely mummy,
When I was little she bought me my dummy.
She's kind and nice and ever so clever,
I'll love always forever and ever.
She's beautiful and pretty,
When she's sad she has my pity.
She has to deal with 5 kids
And undo lots of baby bottle lids.
I love my mummy,
She's ever so funny.
She's a lovely mummy, it's true!

Teri Mayhew (9)
1st Portslade (St Andrews) Brownies

My Mummy

My mummy is the best
She always makes me laugh,
She always makes me nice food.

Keeley Knights (8)
1st Portslade (St Andrews) Brownies

With love

Keeley Knights

Mum

My mum works in Brighton,
She is a nurse,
She spends a lot of money out of her purse,
My mum's favourite animal is a dog,
Me and my mum like hugging logs.

Hannah Oliver (9)
1st Portslade (St Andrews) Brownies

Mum

My mum is the best,
Better than all the rest.
Her favourite animal is a giraffe,
I really like it when she laughs.

Chloe Elliott (10)
1st Portslade (St Andrews) Brownies

Barney

Barney is very good,
She is very kind,
She likes everyone,
She helps if she can
And she is very funny too,
Everyone likes her as much as I do.

Josie Preddy (8)
1st Portslade (St Andrews) Brownies

Brownies

B est thing ever
R ound and round we go
O nly girls!
W ow, wow and wow!
N othing is wrong
I like it
E verthing is right.

Emily Smith (10)
1st Holtspur Brownies, Beaconsfield

Brownies

B rownies is what I think about all day

R unning around hop and play

O n the go all the time

W hatever we do is totally fine

N o one gets bored on Tuesday

 I n our Brownies we like to say

'E xcellent'

S o that is what we do in Brownies.

Tiffany Burnham (10)
1st Holtspur Brownies, Beaconsfield

Mrs Cook

When I am sad Mrs Cook makes me happy.
When I cry Mrs Cook makes me laugh,
And that is how Mrs Cook make me happy and laugh.

Giulia Gibbons (10)
1st Holtspur Brownies, Beaconsfield

Vikky

Vikky is the best,
Travelling north, south, east and west.

When she cuddles me up tight,
She always whispers, 'Good night.'

When I go to bed and rest my head on my pillow,
Every time I think of her I feel like a willow.

When she cooks
She always reads the recipe book.

When she wakes up I think of her a lot,
When I think of her she is a jackpot.

When she sends her love,
She loves me like a dove.

Lindsey Sheffield (9)
1st Holtspur Brownies, Beaconsfield

Miranda

M iranda's magical as can be
I have fun with her all the time
R unning like mad
A great friend
N agging all the time
D a best
A funny friend.

Laura Wheatley (9)
1st Holtspur Brownies, Beaconsfield

Laura

L ovely girl as can be
A s funny as a clown she is
U nhappy when she falls over
R unning very fast
A good friend forever she will be.

Miranda Peacock (9)
1st Holtspur Brownies, Beaconsfield

My Grandma

G randma drives down to see me in her small car
R emembers me at all times
A lways plays with me
N ever lies to me
D oes lots of fun things with me
M akes me smile
A nd I love her very much.

Anna Carter-Roberts (9)
1st Holtspur Brownies, Beaconsfield

Alexandra

Alexandra is a little girl
With wonderful brown eyes
And she loves to smack my bum.
She has got brown hair.
She makes everything fair.
She loves to play with me.
She's a very kind girl.
And she loves to go to bed.
She hates to write poems,
She loves to go to Brownies.

Lulu Pratt (8)
1st Holtspur Brownies, Beaconsfield

My Mum Angie

A ngie Elliott
N icest mum ever
G ood and kind
I s great
E nergetic.

Kelsie Elliott (8)
1st Holtspur Brownies, Beaconsfield

Thomas

T homas is my brother
H e does as he's told by my mother
O bedient Thomas likes to cook
M aking brownies and reading a book
A crobatic Thomas is so great
S o now he has just turned eight.

Alice Devoy (8)
1st Holtspur Brownies, Beaconsfield

Dick And Dom

D is for Dominic
I is for icky
C is for creamy muck
K is for kicking.

A is for absolutely cool
N is for naughty
D is for that dog.

D is for Dick
O is for orange in the fruit bowl
M is for magic.

April Walshaw (8)
1st Holtspur Brownies, Beaconsfield

Lulu

Lulu is a little girl
With wonderful blue eyes
And she loves to scream and play with me.
She has blonde hair,
She makes everything fair.
She is a very kind girl
And she loves to go to Brownies.

Alexandra Baldwin (7)
1st Holtspur Brownies, Beaconsfield

My Grandma

When I was little my grandma read to me,
She read stories like 'Little Red Riding Hood'
'Puss in Boots' and 'Dick Whittington'.

I talk about her in bed,
I like to remember her.

She has grey hair
And wears glasses.

She is the best.

Helen Carter-Roberts (7)
1st Holtspur Brownies, Beaconsfield

Enid Blyton

E nid Blyton is my favourite author,
N ow she has passed away but her books still inspire me,
I like all of her books,
D id the best stories ever.

B owls away the bad dreams at night,
L ove her books do I.
Y ou would be inspired by how she can write,
T o the world of imagination is where her books will take you.
O n I go reading, reading the books that inspire me.
N ever will her books run away from me.

Rebecca Jurdon (7)
1st Holtspur Brownies, Beaconsfield

Mummy

I think my mummy's great,
She gobbles food off her plate.
My mummy is the best in the world,
There's no one else
In the world
That can be better than her.

Sarah Miller (7)
1st Holtspur Brownies, Beaconsfield

Rosamund

R is for Rosamund my best friend
O ff we go together
S is for sweet
A is for always splitting up
M ountains of pleasure
U nicorn friend
N aughty friend
D oing lots of things with me.

Melissa Amery (7)
1st Holtspur Brownies, Beaconsfield

Melissa

M is for Melissa, my best friend
E is for an excellent girl called Melissa
L is for laughing together in the playground
I is for interesting games that Melissa makes up
S is for being silly with Melissa
S is for a sweet voice spoken by Melissa
A is for an angel who is Melissa.

Rosamund Carpenter (7)
1st Holtspur Brownies, Beaconsfield

Untitled

My mum is generous and caring
She is game for a laugh and is very daring
When we go riding she is dancing and cheering
My mum eats pears and likes pair skating
And every day she is always there waiting.

Remi Harvie (8)
10th A Brownie Pack, Irvine

My Granny

She wraps me up in a blanket when I don't feel well.
She makes me hot chocolate.
She looks after my dog.
She makes me laugh and gives me cuddles when I cry.
She spoils me and picks me up from school.
I love my granny.

Katie Little (8)
10th A Brownie Pack, Irvine